Funeral ˈ.

by Pat Wilson

SAMUELFRENCH.COM   SAMUELFRENCH.CO.UK

FOR PRODUCTION ENQUIRIES

UNITED STATES AND CANADA
Info@SamuelFrench.com
1-866-598-8449

UNITED KINGDOM AND EUROPE
Plays@SamuelFrench.co.uk
020-7255-4302

Each title is subject to availability from Samuel French, depending upon country of performance. Please be aware that *FUNERAL TEA* may not be licensed by Samuel French in your territory. Professional and amateur producers should contact the nearest Samuel French office or licensing partner to verify availability.

Please refer to page 22 for further copyright information.

FUNERAL TEA

A One-Act Play

For Five Women

CHARACTERS

MRS. ELLIS . . . . .Who caters privately
for funerals, weddings, etc.

MRS. MURGATROYD . . . . Niece of the departed
Jacob Starkie

MISS STARKIE . . . . Her younger sister

MISS PARKER . . . . Their friend

MRS. BOOTH . . . . . An old lady who just enjoys funerals

TIME: The present.
PLACE: A small town in Yorkshire, England.

3

PRODUCTION NOTE

A Cockney or British accent will enhance the humor of this play but that's only frosting on the cake or perhaps, cream in the tea. The lines can be delivered in plain American if they come across more successfully or the actors are more comfortable in the performance.

A detailed prop list is included in the back of the play book.

FUNERAL TEA

SCENE: The front parlor of a modest house in a York-shire town.   The furniture is well-worn conventional.   A table holds ample refreshments and china.   Various chairs are near the table.   A sideboard is stage L. and a fireplace R.

AT RISE OF CURTAIN: MRS. ELLIS enters with a plate of party sandwiches.   She places it tastefully on the table with the rest of the repast.   Then she goes to the sideboard, picks up a large spray of flowers, looks at the black-edged card and sighs.   Takes a spray out with reverence, returns immediately.   Tidies hearth, plumps up cushions.   Goes to sideboard cupboard.   Finds it locked.   Tries door again to make sure.   Shakes her head and goes off as sound of car stopping is heard.   MISS STARKIE, MISS PARKER and MRS. BOOTH enter.   They wear sedate dress and hats suitable for a funeral.   All have handkerchiefs which they use to dry their eyes.   MRS. MURGATROYD'S voice is heard off.

MRS. MURGATROYD.   [Off]   Aye well . . . you'll
    come back for us in an hour won't you lad?   I'm

right sorry you won't come in for a cup of tea, but it was a right nice ride in your fine limousine. You Mr. Thakery, 'as done everything very nice too. Aye . I'll see to yon . . .

[The others examine the table, take off their gloves and coats but not their hats. MRS. ELLIS enters rather out of breath just as MRS. MURGATROYD finishes with limousine. The one follows the other in]

MRS. ELLIS. [To MRS. M.] Ee luv, you're back in good time . . . I've just finished t'table.
MISS PARKER. And very nice too. [Approvingly]
MRS. ELLIS. [Preening] Aye. I do all t'funeral teas, an' weddin's if they want them done private, like . . . but mind you, I've niver done a creemation affore. [The ladies look as if they are royalty] I usually does funerals in 'am, but I felt it didn't fit wi' a creemation, . . . So I've done chicken and cucumber. [The ladies are suitably impressed]
MRS. MURGATROYD. And very nice too. A very nice thought. I see what you mean.
MRS. ELLIS. T'paper napkins as you 'ad in t'drawer 'ad a "Merry Christmas" on 'em. So I made so bold as to buy a packet from t'corner shop . . .wi' violets on t'corners. Violets being more appropriate like . . . being purple . . . sort of half mourning.
MISS STARKIE. Very touching I'm sure. I can see you understand. You must be proper used to it.
MRS. ELLIS. [Smoothing her white uniform] Oh aye . . . Highly recommended.
MRS. MURGATROYD. [Tentatively] As there is only four of us, mebbee you'd sit down an' 'ave a bite an' sup wi' us?
MRS. ELLIS. [Hastily] Noa . . . Noa . . . I knows

me place. It wouldn't do to sit down wi' t'mourners.
[The ladies feel the dignity of their position and dab at
their eyes]

MRS. BOOTH. All very right and proper. [Pause]

MRS. ELLIS. Well . . . I'll go an' make tea, if you ladies will sit down. [She motions them to the table,
puts their chairs under them and goes off, leaving the
ladies sitting on the edge of their seats]

MISS STARKIE. Well it were quite nice, but all t'same
I'd rather 'ave 'ad Uncle Jacob buried in Topcliff Ceme-
tary. There's room for one more in t'family plot.
One more place affor it's full. [Sighs]

MRS. MURGATROYD. [Kindly] You can 'ave it
Sarah.

MISS STARKIE. [Sharply] You're t'eldest . . . you
should have it by rights.

MRS. MURGATROYD. Noa. I'll lie wi' Sam. We're
putting a bit by for our own sma plot.

MISS STARKIE. [Pensively] I don't know as 'ow I
hold wi' all these modern ideas, but . . . Uncle Jacob
paid into t'creemation club 'ee can 'ave things as 'ee
wanted them.

MISS PARKER. [Unbending a bit and inspecting the
table] Well . . . you've done 'im very well wi' t'tea.
A fancy spread.

MRS. MURGATROYD. [Pondering] Jacob allus had a
craze for clubs. 'ee were always in t'Christmas club,
and Rotary club. But 'ee didn't know what 'ee were
letting 'isself inffor when 'ee joined this one!

MISS STARKIE. Aye . . . It's a pity there weren't more
folks to come, but we've lost touch, since urban re-
newal re-housed us. We knows no one up 'ere.
Mind . . . I'm not saying it's not very handy havin' a
bath . . . an' gas stove. But it's noan so friendly as
living in t'owld building, like when we were in t'school.

MRS. BOOTH. Aye . . . an' we're none of us as chummy

as we were.

[Enter MRS. ELLIS with large tea pot and starts to pour out]

MRS. ELLIS.   I'm sorry I've been so long, girls.   I couldn't find the tea jar.   Do you all take milk and sugar?   [They all assent, are served and sip their tea with great delicacy, little fingers well out]

MRS. ELLIS.   [Handing a plate of sandwiches to MRS. BOOTH]   I don't think I've 'ad the pleasure of meeting you affor Mrs. er . . . er . . .

MRS. BOOTH.   Booth is the name.

MRS. MURGATROYD.   I presume you were a friend of Uncle Jacob's, Mrs. Booth?

MRS. BOOTH.   Noa . . . I niver met 'im   . . . at least I don't think so.   Though it's more than likely that I did, as I'm sixty-seven, an' accordin' to t'notice in t'paper 'ee were seventy.

MISS STARKIE.   Aye that's right.   Seventy come Christmas.

MRS. BOOTH.   It said in t'memoriam 'ee worked in t'mill.   An' I were a doffer before I were laid off.   [Pause]   Aah always goes to funerals.   You have to take your pleasures where you can when you are on the pension.

MISS PARKER.   [Pondering on this]   Well I can't see the 'arm.   An' it filled t'limousine up.   An' I must say you paid your respects very kindly.   And 'aving a older lady with us did add tone.

MRS. ELLIS   [Handing round more food to party which is relaxing a little]   I always goes to t'church to see 'weddings, do you Mrs. Booth?

MRS. BOOTH.   [Inspecting all the cakes one by one before taking one]   Noa, I think nowt to weddings, one bride in white is t'same as another.   Noa, funerals is much more interesting . . . besides, you get

a free tea. But I must say I've niver been to a creemation affor.

MRS. ELLIS. [Mysteriously to MRS. M.] Was it very . . .
er . . .?

MRS. MURGATROYD. [Offhand] Nay . . . we saw
nowt. But it was right funny us going twice.

MRS. BOOTH. Twice? That was queer!

MISS STARKIE. Aye, it was. We went to t'service
on Monday and then t'Lawyer said we 'ad to go today to get t'remains . . . according to Jacob's Will.

MRS. BOOTH. I thought it were quick! We were sort of
in, an' then we were out! But havin' the limousine twice
must 'a' cost deal of cash!

MISS STARKIE. [With dignity] All provided for . . .
all provided for in Uncle Jacob's Will. Creemation,
one day, an' then ashes to be scattered later.

MRS. BOOTH. Well now . . .it were very kind o' 'im
to provide for two rides. Er . . did you 'ave two teas?

MRS. MURGATROYD. Nay, we just 'as a cuppa coffee
at t'Co-op first time.

MRS. BOOTH. Oh! I must 'ave missed that!

MRS. MURGATROYD. [To MRS. ELLIS] Do 'ave a
cup o' tea, Mrs. Ellis.

MRS. ELLIS. [Firmly] Noa . . . I 'ave mine when you're
gone. An' then I'll leave all tidy and make fire up.
Shall I mash another pot?

MISS PARKER. [Looking in teapot] It could do wi'
another spoonful of tea.

MRS. ELLIS. [Taking teapot] Aye, well t'kettle's on
t'boil, an' I've got plenty of tea now.

[She trots off and returns quickly. While she is
away, MRS. BOOTH inspects every sandwich and
finally selects one]

MRS. ELLIS. [Pouring out fresh tea] You weren't
away long. You were very quick.

MRS. MURGATROYD. [Rather disgruntled] Aye it were. An' we'd no time to enjoy the ride . . . an' nobody saw us. We did stop at t'traffic light, but nobody saw us there, but t'minister's wife, and she keeps herself to herself, more's the pity.

MISS STARKIE. An' I brought this 'at specially to show my respects for Uncle Jacob.

MISS PARKER. I never wore a hat, before, neither, but it do seem so proper for a funeral.

MRS. BOOTH. When I were young we wore shawls. They was very 'andy for slippin' on an' slippin' out. An' there's nowt like a shawl for carryin' a baby. You can lap it up tight in t'shawl an' then hold it fast to your 'ip an' then lap yourself up in t'shawl.

MRS. ELLIS. [Handing cakes to MRS. BOOTH, who takes one, but puts it back, having reached the Plimsoll mark] Have you had a family Mrs. Booth?

MRS. BOOTH. Aye, I 'as a lad in Canada. But I doubt I shall ever see 'im again. It's ower far away. But 'ee sends me a Christmas card . . . I misses t'auld days.

MISS PARKER. My mum said there were more to do. There were t'Great West Riding galas. Do you remember t'fireworks? An' t'man as went up in a ballon.

MRS. MURGATROYD. Aye! I remember 'im going up. Did 'ee iver come down?

MISS STARKIE. Not as I iver heard me mum say.

MRS. MURGATROYD. T'things I misses most is t'trams. Took 'em away when I was eight. We couldn't sleep. Used to lie awake at night listening for them not coming! [They sit and ponder]

MRS. BOOTH. Aye well . . . they'm gone, like poor Jacob.

MRS. MURGATROYD. [Still pondering] I wonder why 'ee wanted 'is dust 'an ashes scattered on t'cricket field.

MISS STARKIE. Why, 'ee were a great man for sports were Uncle Jacob.

MRS. MURGATROYD. [Ruminating] I don't know as 'ow 'ee were really. 'ee were a bit vindictive were Jacob. 'ee allus liked a game best if someone got hurt. No 'arm as you might say, but all t'same . . .

MISS STARKIE. Aye, mebbee you're right Martha. But we must not speak ill o' the dead.

MRS. MURGATROYD. Nay, nay, thu's right. But 'ee did enjoy a bit of a calamity you know. 'ee were right pleased when t'bomb fell on t'station. 'ee couldn't get down quick enough to see t'damage.

MISS STARKIE. Aye, an' 'ee were right put out when 'ee found Willie Jackson were on t'other shift!

MRS. BOOTH. Ee! Fancy that!

MISS PARKER. All t'same, 'ee did like watching t'cricket. 'ee allus struck up for Yorkshire. Liked to watch 'em bat.

MRS. MURGATROYD. Especially if someone got a bat in t'eye.

MRS. ELLIS. [Filling in an awkward silence] Do you think you ladies could do wi' another cup? I'll boil t'kettle again. Pot 'ull stand another watering.

MRS. MURGATROYD. Aye, do. We will an' all. Funerals is thirsty work.

MRS. ELLIS. Well you'll just have time affor you go. [Exits to kitchen]

MRS. BOOTH. It's nice to be waited on. I've done nowt today but make me bed. I allus makes me bed, because I allus thinks if I were to 'ave an accident, an' be brought home dead it would be right comforting to know as t'bed were made.

MRS. MURGATROYD. Aye, you can't be too careful.

MISS STARKIE. O'course if you 'ad an accident you'd be taken to t'Hospital.

MRS. BOOTH. Oh Aye . . . and they allus 'as beds made up there, stands to reason . . . But this is a nice sup o' tea. It makes a pleasant change.

MISS PARKER. I still keep wondering why Mr. Starkie wanted 'is ashes scattered on t'cricket field.

MISS STARKIE. [Forgetting herself] Maybe so as Yorkshire would get t'ashes! [They others look shocked] Well Jacob wouldn't do owt for nowt. Mebbee 'ee wanted everyone to get dust in their eyes.

MRS. MURGATROYD. [Annoyed] Sarah! I knew you an Uncle Jacob niver saw eye to eye, but shouldn't niver 'ave that sort o' talk, an' 'im not cold.

MISS STARKIE. Well 'ee should be, 'ee been done over three days! [The others regard her in stony silence] And now wear'st flowers? T'Club sent a nice spray, an I've just remembered. They should be on t'table.

MRS. MURGATROYD. I don't know. We was to 'ave taken them to t'Hospital on way back from t'scatterin'.

MISS STARKIE. Well we didn't take them to t'creemation.

MISS PARKER. [Getting up and looking round room] Well they are here . . . When we've finished tea we might go an stand round t'coffin. I allus thinks it's the proper thing to do.

MRS. MURGATROYD. [Slightly bewildered] Coffin? Urn?

MISS STARKIE. We haven't got one! [They all look at each other]

MRS. BOOTH [After deep thought] Why, t'Undertaker will bring it back.

MISS STARKIE. Did 'ee say so?

MRS. MURGATROYD. Noa, 'ee said 'ee wouldn't be back.

MISS STARKIE. Well where is it? We brought nothing back wi' us!

MISS PARKER. Noa . . . that's right, there was only us, and t'driver and t'Undertaker in front of t' limousine an' 'ee didn't come back wi' us.

MRS. MURGATROYD. We left it!

MISS STARKIE. [Getting excited] That's just like Uncle Jacob! To get 'is self lost! I remember when he took us to the fireworks we niver saw sight or sound of him fra' t'bus gettin' us thear to us finding 'im to go home.

MRS. MURGATROYD. [Hotly] I doant think it decent to talk about getting lost at t' fireworks under present circumstances.

[Enter MRS. ELLIS with fresh tea]

MRS. ELLIS. [Briskly pouring out] Now if you ladies will sup up I think it will be time for you to get ready for your last sad duty.

[They all sit speechless at MRS. ELLIS bustles out]

MRS. MURGATROYD. [Glumly supping her tea] I don't know what we are going to say to 'er.

MISS PARKER. [Also drinking] There must 'ave been summat somewhere.

MRS. MURGATROYD. I remember summat. After we'd waited t'Undertaker gave me a sort of tea jar thing . . . but I thought nowt to it. I put it . . . [Look of horror crosses her face — she looks at the other, and MRS. BOOTH chokes into her cup]

MISS STARKIE.   [Hysterically]   We've drunk Uncle Jacob!
Mrs. Ellis said she couldn't find t'tea jar.

MRS. MURGATROYD.   I shall niver sleep again!

MRS. BOOTH.   [Getting up and making ready to leave]
And I shall niver drink tea again.   I'm going home.
This 'as fair knocked the bottom out of me for going
to creemations.   I'm going to stick to funerals in
future.

MRS. MURGATROYD.   [Stopping her]   Nay, nay,
you mustn't go.   We must stick together.   We must
have a plan.

MRS. BOOTH.   [Faintly]   Nay luv, I'm going!   I've
'ad a right belly full!

MISS STARKIE.   [Even more hysterical]   That's a
right gruesome thing to say.   [Stands up and staggers
about]   Oh dear!   Oh dear!

MRS. MURGATROYD.   [Going to her]   She's going
to 'ave one of her turns.   Give 'er some brandy,
it's in t'sideboard.

MISS PARKER.   [Rattling the sideboard door]   It's
locked, Martha.

MRS. MURGATROYD.   [Fanning MISS STARKIE with
a napkin]   Well gi' 'er a sup o' 'of tea, then.
[MRS. BOOTH picks up teapot]

MISS STARKIE.   [Almost in a frenzy]   Don't touch
t'teapot!   It's full o' Jacob Starkie!   Oh!   Oh!   Oh!
I shall go stark staring mad!

MISS PARKER.   [Still trying to open cupboard door]
Why is sideboard locked?

MISS STARKIE.   [Between gasps]   I locked it, I put
t'bit of insurance money in it, and I locked t'door
affor we went out.

MRS. MURGATROYD.   [Hollowly]   Then it must be true.
We must a' drunk Uncle Jacob, for t'tea were in t'side-
board cupboard.   We allus keeps it there . . . I told
Mrs Ellis.

MISS PARKER. You must have given it to 'er affor we went to t'creemation, and you've forgotten.

MRS. MURGATROYD. Noa! Noa! I may a' given it 'er after we came back. Can't remember what I did affor we went.

MRS. BOOTH. Well for heaven's sake, get sideboard open and then we'll know.

MISS PARKER. Aye, and if t'tea jars not there, we'll be all right. Where's t'key?

MRS' MURGATROYD. [To MISS STARKIE] You 'ave.

MISS STARKIE. [Faintly] I can't remember where I put it. [They all frantically rummage in her bag]

MRS. MURGATROYD. Well look in your 'andbag, you great gorp.

MISS PARKER. Look in your pocket. [More frantic searching]

MRS. MURGATROYD. You may 'ave dropped it.

MISS STARKIE. Nay, I don't think so, unless it's on t'floor. [Everybody crawls about searching and getting very dishevelled]

MISS STARKIE. [Suddenly from her hands and knees] I've remembered.

MRS. BOOTH. Well whear is it?

MISS STARKIE. It's in t'heavenly door.

MRS. MURGATROYD. Have you gone off your head, Sarah?

MRS. BOOTH. T'strain's been too much for 'er. She's gone off 'er chump. [Shakes her head sadly]

MISS STARKIE. Noa I 'aven't. I put it in my hymn book to mark t'place in case we sang t'hymn again.
"T'heavenly gates were open wide
And angel voice said come."

MRS. MURGATROYD. It weren't t'heavenly gates as opened for Uncle Jacob.

MISS PARKER. Noa, an' I don't think much o' t'choice o' t'hymn.

MISS STARKIE. Well it were better an' more appro-
    priate than Uncle's favourite, which were "For those
    in peril on the sea". [She gets hysterical again]
    It should 'a' been, for those in peril in the tea!
MRS. MURGATROYD. SARAH!
MISS PARKER. You better go an' lie down.
MRS. BOOTH. Nay, let's get t'sideboard open first.
MISS PARKER. Aye, whear's t'hymn book?
MISS STARKIE. [Fumbling in coat pocket] 'ee
    it is, an' 'ere's t'key.
MRS. BOOTH. Ee, I do hope that tea is not in t'side-
    board. [They watch in horrified silence as MRS.
    M. unlocks the door]
MRS. MURGATROYD. IT IS! [She removes jar, which
    is a large old-fashioned vase type, or similar]
MISS STARKIE. [In awe-struck tones] We've drunk 'im!
    An' we've nowt to take to t'cricket ground.
MRS. MURGATROYD. Well we must face facts. T'neigh-
    bours will expect to see summat when we go out.
MISS PARKER. Aye we must take summat to t'cricket
    ground to scatter. Anything.
MRS. BOOTH. [Inspired] We could take t'teapot.
MRS. MURGATROYD. Nowt o' t'sort. That teapot
    was give to me by Murgatroyd . . . besides, a fine lot
    of fooils we'd look, plonking a teapot on t' cricket
    pitch!
MISS PARKER. A silly carry on . . .
MISS STARKIE. At silly mid-off!
MRS. MURGATROYD. Sarah! Pull yourself to-
    gether.
MRS. BOOTH. I shall niver drink tea again as long
    as I live! Ee, I do wish I'd niver come! It isn't as
    if I rightly knowed 'im.
MISS STARKIE. [Nastily] Well now, you're getting
    inside information. [Wildly] Oh, what are we goin'
    to do? We can't walk out wi' nowt! And neigh-

bours all gorping.   Jacob only got creemated to spite us all . . . and cucumber doesn't agree wi' me.   [Wails] Martha, what are we to do?

MRS. MURGATROYD.   Control yourself, Sarah!   Well now, we must take some ashes out o' t'hearth and put them in a box and make some sort of a show.   Sarah, you find a box, luv.

MISS STARKIE.   [Scuttling to sideboard]   There's a chocolate box, but it 'as 'Present from Blackpool' on it.

MISS PARKER.   I thinks you wants a jar, a cookie jar or a toffee candy jor or summat.   [MISS STARKIE picks up a jar and gazes at it fascinatedly]

MRS. MURGATROYD.   What's up with you now?

MISS STARKIE.   It says 'Creamola Toffee'.

MRS. MURGATROYD.   [Snapping]   Well what does thu expect it to say?   Cinder toffee?

MISS PARKER.   Don't you start!   Sarah, get that jar emptied.

MISS STARKIE.   [Getting very agitated, with a hand pushed down into jar.   It's got a lot of toffee inside.   [Struggles furiously]

MISS PARKER.   Well doant lose your 'ead.

MISS STARKIE.   [trying to free her hand]   I haven't lost me 'ead, its me 'and.   It's stuck in t'jar.   [Notices MARTHA grovelling by fireplace] What are you doing, Martha?

MRS. MURGATROYD.   Trying to get some ashes, but she's left noan!   She's too blooming thorough!   What she want to take all t'ashes away for?

MISS STARKIE.   [Pulling hand free of jar, putting it down on table and getting it stuck to paper napkin] To make herself a nice pot of tea, I shouldn't wonder.

MRS. BOOTH.   [In sepulchral voice]   That teapot's givin' me the creeps.   I once went to a fillum called Christmas Carol, and a door knocker turned into the

ghost of Jacob Marley. And that teapot is turning into
the ghost of Jacob Starkie! I can feel t'room growin'
cold . . .

MRS. MURGATROYD. [Snappily] Well put your coat
on, put some coal on, an' 'old your tongue. T'limousine will be 'ere in a minute.

MISS STARKIE. But whear'st flowers? THEY can't
'ave been spirited away!

MRS. BOOTH. [Glumly] I wish I were spirited away.
I came out for a pleasant time an' a good cry, an' now
I'm scared to go home, and scared to stop 'ere.

MISS PARKER. I know I shall hear things that go bump
in the neet.

[There is a bump outside, MRS. P. and MRS. B.
clutch each other, MRS. MURGATROYD collapses
in a chair, a car horn sounds off stage and MISS STAR-
KIE dives under table. MRS. ELLIS enters, carrying
a urn and spray of flowers. She puts both on table,
bends down and looks at MISS STARKIE.]

MISS STARKIE. [Crawling out] I, I've lost me hymn
book, I mean I've lost Uncle Jacob.

MRS. ELLIS. [Kindly] Not lost, but gone before.
Now, if you ladies will arrange yourselves . . . if Mrs.
Murgatroyd were to walk wi' Miss Starkie, an' carry
t'flowers . . . [She arranges them in front of table,
hands flowers to MRS. M. who promptly drops them.
She gives them back to MRS. M.] And if Mrs. Booth
and Mrs. Parker were to walk behind an' I were to
follow wi' t'remains, it would look very nice for t'neigh-
bours.

MRS. MURGATROYD. Wi' t'remains?

MRS. ELLIS. Aye, t'Undertaker gave me t'casket an'
I put it in t'front bedroom wi' t'flowers in front o'
it. All very proper.

MISS STARKIE. [In a daze] All very proper!
MISS PARKER. 'Ighly recommended!
MRS. BOOTH. Aye . . .
MRS. ELLIS. [Briskly] Well, ladies, shall we go?
I can clear up after I've seen you into t'limousine.
Oh! and you've got t'cupboard door opens. Couldn't
find t'key anywhere, so I couldn't get t'tea, and that
reminds me. Mrs. Murgatroyd, you owe me eight
pence. I slipped out for a quarter of tea, as I didn't
want to bother you. Folks don't want upsetting at
a time like this.
MRS. MURGATROYD. Very good of you, I'm sure.

[They trail out in procession, MRS. ELLIS fusses
around, picks up tea jar and follows them. Noises
off of car doors slamming and car starting off.
MRS. E. returns, sits down and pours out a cup
of tea. Sips it]

MRS. ELLIS. Eugh! Cold as the grave. I'll make
some fresh. [She picks up casket, looks in horror
at it, puts it down again, picks it up, runs to door,
shouting] Martha – Sarah, come back. You've
gone wi' out Uncle Jacob!

CURTAIN

PRODUCTION NOTES

NOTES ON COSTUMES

MISS STARKIE, MISS BOOTH and MRS. MURGATROYD wear plain and not very fashionable clothing subdued enough for a funeral. They have coats and hats. MRS. BOOTH is much older and probably manages a black dress.

MISS ELLIS wears a white uniform with apron or something suggesting cateress.

GLOSSARY

As use is made of some unfamiliar words, the following may be of help:

'Mash'	To brew tea
'Doffer'	Worker in woolen mill
'Lap'	To wrap up
'Fooils'	Fools
'Gorping'	Staring
'Neet'	Night

PRODUCTION NOTES

PROP LIST

Any usual modest furniture but the following must be included:
a sideboard with cupboard, a table & four chairs, arranged
so that no one sits with her back to front stage.

Fireplace, brush & shovel or dustpan.
A coat stand or something suitable to hold wraps.

On sideboard a spray of flowers with black-edged card.
In sideboard drawer paper napkins with violets.
In sideboard cupboard the **tea jar.**
On sideboard a candy jar.
On table a cloth set diagonally & fully set for the meal.
Must look quite lavish.

Teapot.
The **Urn,** which must resemble the **tea jar** to some extent,
near enough to be confusing, anyway.
A hymn book with key in it, is in the pocket of MISS
STARKIE'S coat.
Handkerchiefs for the ladies.

MUSIC USE NOTE

Licensees are solely responsible for obtaining formal written permission from copyright owners to use copyrighted music in the performance of this play and are strongly cautioned to do so. If no such permission is obtained by the licensee, then the licensee must use only original music that the licensee owns and controls. Licensees are solely responsible and liable for all music clearances and shall indemnify the copyright owners of the play(s) and their licensing agent, Samuel French, against any costs, expenses, losses and liabilities arising from the use of music by licensees. Please contact the appropriate music licensing authority in your territory for the rights to any incidental music.

IMPORTANT BILLING AND CREDIT REQUIREMENTS

If you have obtained performance rights to this title, please refer to your licensing agreement for important billing and credit requirements.

Lightning Source UK Ltd.
Milton Keynes UK
UKHW050848050120
356223UK00008B/153/P

9 780874 408904